Zoom Out!

Ben Hubbard

Houghton Mifflin Harcourt

Zoom Out! was originally published in English in 2016. This edition is published by arrangement with Oxford University Press.

Printed in China

ISBN 978-0-358-26273-2

1 2 3 4 5 6 7 8 9 10 XXXX 28 27 26 25 24 23 22 21 20 19

4500000000 A B C D E F G

Acknowledgments

Series Editor: Nikki Gamble
Cover photo: Baris Simsek/Getty Images & Srdjan111/Shutterstock
Back cover photo: Corbis/ESA/Hubble Collaboration/Handout/CNP

The publisher would like to thank the following for permission to reproduce photographs: **p1:** Corbis/ESA/Hubble Collaboration/Handout/CNP; **p2–3:** Corbis/Ugo Mellone/SOPA RF; **p4–5:** Science Photo Library/Louise Hughes; **p5b:** Alamy/Mark Eveleigh, Getty Images/Antagain; **p6–7:** Alamy/Mark Eveleigh, Getty Images/Antagain; **p7t:** Nature Picture Library/Warwick Sloss; **p7b:** Getty Images/Danita Delimont; **p8:** Nature Picture Library/Andy Rouse; **p8–9:** Getty Images/Danita Delimont; **p9b:** Beverly Joubert/Getty Images; **p10–11:** Beverly Joubert/Getty Images; **p10t:** Mogens Trolle/Shutterstock; **p10b:** Maggy Meyer/Shutterstock; **p11t:** Corbis/DLILLC; **p11b:** Getty Images/UIG; **p12:** Getty Images/UIG; **p13t:** Eugene Kalenkovich/Shutterstock; **p13b:** Getty Images/alxpin; **p14–15:** Getty Images/alxpin; **p15:** Getty Images/alxpin; **p16:** Corbis/ESA/Hubble Collaboration/Handout/CNP.

Houghton Mifflin Harcourt Publishing Company
125 High Street
Boston, MA 02110
www.hmhco.com

Contents

An Eye

What is this?

It is an eye!

It is made up of **thousands** of tiny eyes.

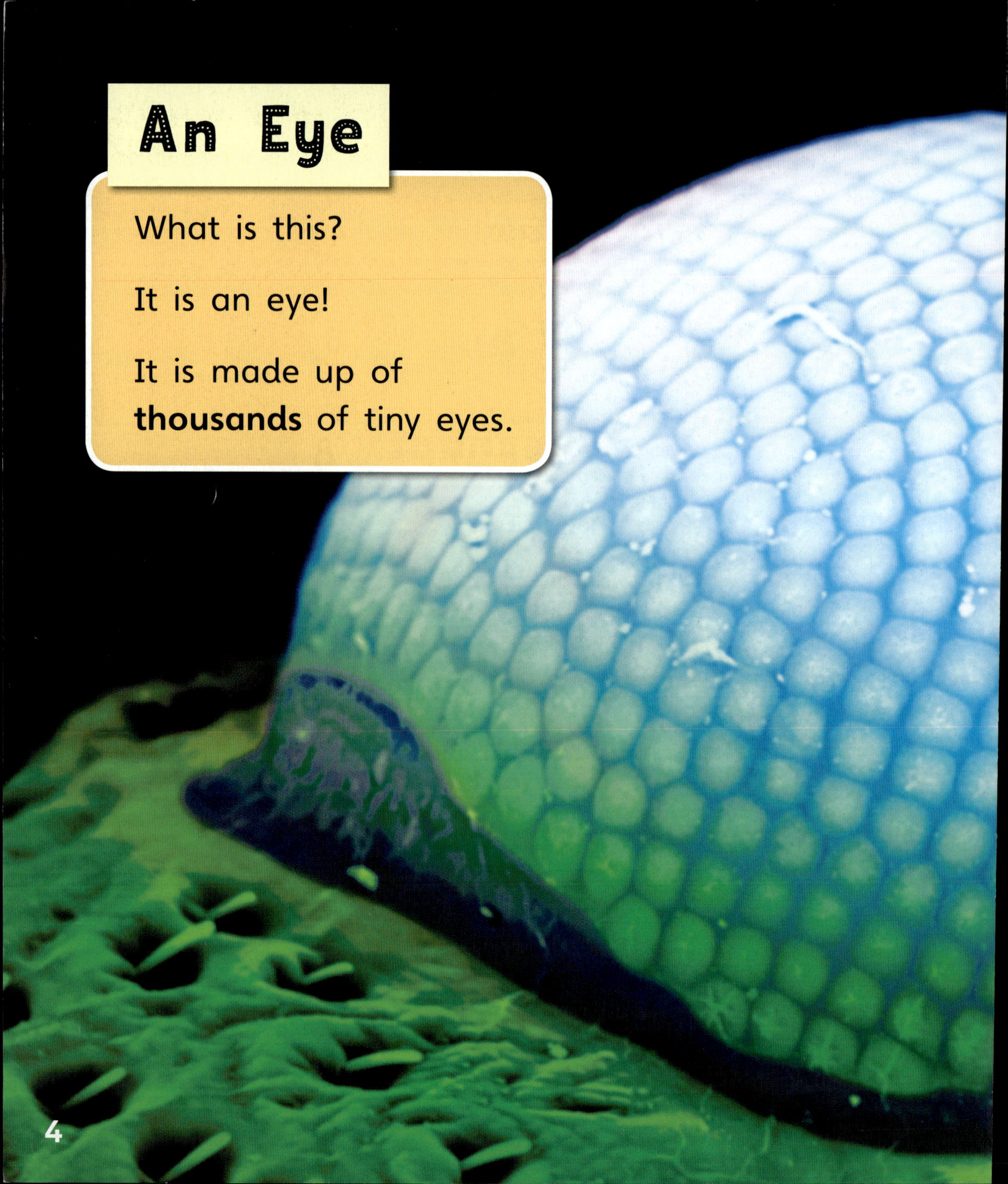

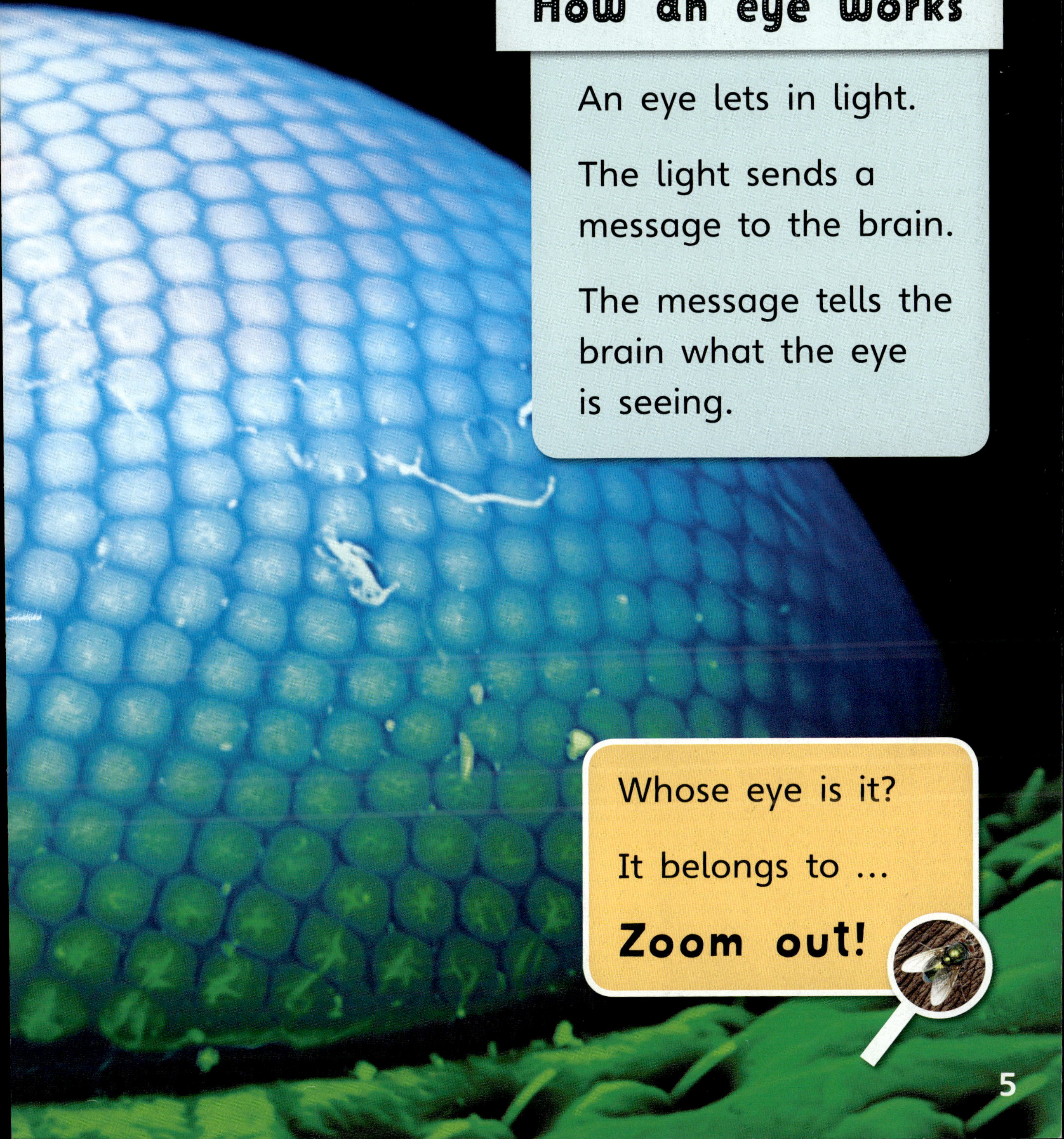

How an eye works

An eye lets in light.

The light sends a message to the brain.

The message tells the brain what the eye is seeing.

Whose eye is it?

It belongs to …

Zoom out!

A Fly

A fly has two buzzing wings and six sticky feet.

This means it can land anywhere – and on anything.

How flies eat

Did you know that flies taste with their feet?

But they can't eat solid food.

They have to spit on food to make it liquid.

Then they suck up the liquid food. Their mouths are shaped like straws!

Where has this fly landed?

It has landed on ...

Zoom out!

An Elephant

Elephants are the largest animals on land.

They have thick, wrinkled skin.

Elephants spray their skin with mud. This keeps them cool in the sun.

Elephant herds

A family of elephants is called a **herd.**

A mother elephant leads the herd from place to place.

The herd is looking for shade, water, and food.

Where is this elephant?

It is in ...

Zoom out!

Kenya

Kenya is a hot country.

It has many amazing wild animals.

As well as elephants, there are animals like rhinos, zebras, and lions.

Kenya also has more than one thousand types of bird.

Kenyan people

Some Kenyan people live in big, busy cities. Others, like the **Maasai** people, live on the **plains**.

Some animals from the plains are dangerous, such as lions and leopards.

There are fences around the Maasai villages to keep out dangerous animals.

Where is Kenya?

It is in ...

Zoom out!

Africa

The **continent** of Africa is very big and very hot.

It has **deserts**, plains, mountains, and forests. There are 55 different countries in Africa.

Over one **billion** people live there.

Land and sea

Africa is the second biggest continent in the world.

There are seven continents in total.

A continent is an area of land where we live.

However, most of the world is sea.

Where is Africa?

It is on ...

Zoom out!

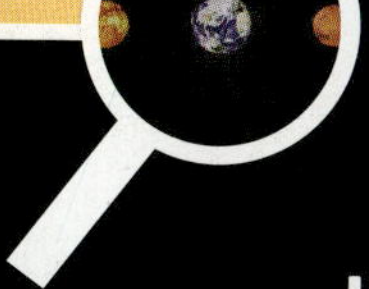

Earth

Our world is the **planet** Earth.

From space, all of the sea makes Earth look blue.

Earth is one of the eight planets in the **solar system**.

Together, these planets circle around the sun.

If you zoomed out more, the solar system would seem small.

The planets would look tiny, like the eyes of a fly!

The universe

You could keep zooming out from the solar system.

Then you would go further out into the **universe**.

You could go on zooming out forever.

You would never reach the end.

Glossary

billion: one thousand million (1,000,000,000)

continent: a huge area of land that can include many different countries

deserts: areas of land with very little rainfall and few plants

herd: a group of animals

Maasai: a group of people who live in Kenya and Tanzania

plains: large areas of flat countryside with few trees

planet: a large ball of rock or gas that revolves around a star

solar system: a sun and the planets that revolve around it

thousands: numbers such as 3,000 or 6,000

universe: the stars, the planets, and everything that exists

Index